Short-Term Memory Difficulties in Children

A practical resource

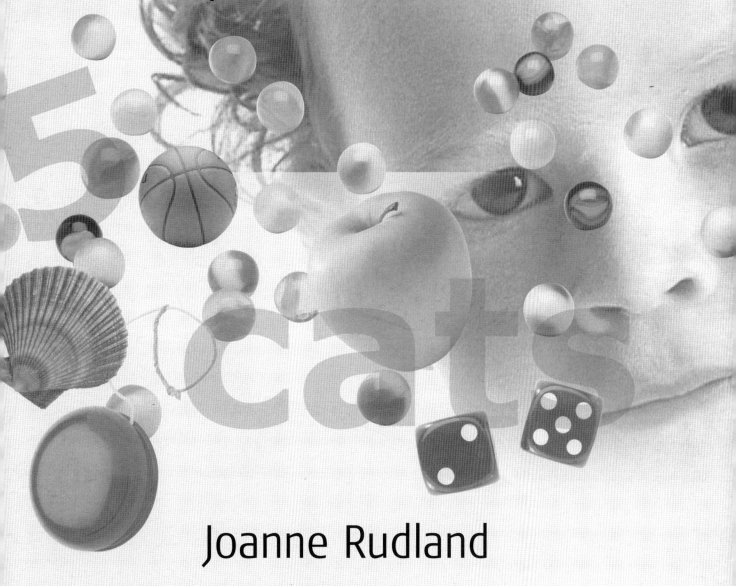

Joanne Rudland

Speechmark

For the purposes of clarity alone, in this text 'he' is used to refer to the client, and 'she' to refer to the therapist.

This book is dedicated to the memory of my grandad,
Walter Rudland ...

First published in 2004 by
Speechmark Publishing Ltd, 70 Alston Drive, Bradwell Abbey, Milton Keynes MK13 9HG, UK
www.speechmark.net

© Joanne Rudland, 2004
Reprinted 2005, 2007, 2008

002-5143/Printed in the United Kingdom/1010

British Library Cataloguing in Publication Data
Rudland, Joanne
  Short-term memory difficulties in children. – (A Speechmark practical therapy resource)
  1. Memory disorders   2. Memory in children   3. Short-term memory
  I. Title
  618.9'283

ISBN 978 0 86388 441 2

Contents

Preface

SHORT-TERM MEMORY DIFFICULTIES IN CHILDREN has been designed for speech and language therapists currently supporting children with short-term memory difficulties. Educational psychologists and learning support teachers may also find parts of this book useful. Activities is this book are aimed at seven- to eleven-year-olds whose short-term memory difficulties have a negative impact on language comprehension and learning.

Due to its nature, this programme cannot meet the needs of those children who have poor attention and/or disordered language skills. With sensitive adaptation, clinicians may find aspects of the programme useful in helping children with dyslexia to develop their awareness of memory.

The resource provides a structured yet flexible programme of graded activities, useful in teaching and practising memory strategies. The programme can be administered in its entirety, or as an accompaniment to clinicians' existing packages of care, and is best suited to individual intervention.

Chapter 1
An introduction to memory theory

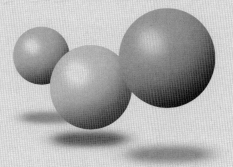

Early Contributors to Memory Theory

Memory research has a long and important history within psychology.

(Hayes, 2002, p64)

One of the most respected and influential figures in the study of memory is that of a German psychologist, Hermann Ebbinghaus. Ebbinghaus (1885/1964) took a particular interest in memory in its purest form, and conducted his work through highly controlled experiments. These experiments were carefully designed to remove as many influencing variables to learning and recall as possible. Ebbinghaus conducted the experiments on himself, and his research involved 'memorising long lists of nonsense syllables' (Bourtchouladze, 2002, p8), to enable him to monitor his own ability to learn and recall.

Ebbinghaus' work acknowledged that:
- memory involves three processes: encoding, storage and retrieval;
- memory fades with time – this is known as the 'curve of forgetting theory';
- repeating information can prolong its existence within memory.

Another important and respected name within the field of memory research is that of Sir Frederick Bartlett (1932/1995), whose work was in stark contrast to that of Ebbinghaus. Bartlett was particularly interested in finding out how memory functioned in the real world. His 'serial reproduction method' involved subjects listening to, or reading, a story. Subjects were then asked to retell the story from memory. The experiment allowed Bartlett to develop his understanding of memory by studying the types of errors commonly made by subjects during recall. Bartlett's work acknowledged that:
- memory is an active process (rather than a passive process that simply soaks up information and reproduces it, like for like);
- accuracy in recall is significantly reduced when information is unfamiliar or incoherent to the subject.

The Characteristics of Memory

It is now widely accepted that memory consists of three kinds of store: the sensory memory store, the short-term/working memory store and the long-term memory store.

```
┌──────────────────────────────────────┐
│         SENSORY MEMORY STORE          │
└──────────────────────────────────────┘

┌──────────────────────────────────────┐
│    SHORT-TERM/WORKING MEMORY STORE    │
└──────────────────────────────────────┘

┌──────────────────────────────────────┐
│        LONG-TERM MEMORY STORE         │
└──────────────────────────────────────┘
```

Sensory Memory

Sometimes referred to as the 'sensory register', 'sensory buffer store' or 'sensory storage', the sensory memory is believed to actively store incoming information from the body's sensory organs. Only a fraction of the incoming information will be acknowledged and directed into the short-term memory. Information lasts approximately one to four seconds in the sensory memory before evaporating: some psychologists consider this process to be part of sensory perception, rather than a form of memory.

Short-Term Memory (STM)

The STM is also referred to as the 'primary memory', 'immediate memory', or 'short-term store'. The term 'working memory' is often used to describe the specific mechanics of STM. Here, the information is stored on a temporary basis. Up to seven pieces of information at a time can be retained for approximately 20 seconds. By implementing specific memory strategies, the STM can be manipulated, and its performance enhanced: the development of these strategies is the focus of this book.

STM is very fragile, and the information within it evaporates as and when direct attention is re-directed or disrupted. Tasks such as carrying out mental arithmetic, responding to a verbal question, and memorising a telephone number from a phone book whilst dialling, all rely on STM.

Long-Term Memory (LTM)

Also referred to as the 'secondary memory', 'distant memory' or 'long-term store', the LTM is a vast store that holds learnt knowledge and past life experiences. LTM retains all those 'things in memory which are not currently being used, but which are potentially retrievable' (Gross, 1989). It is estimated that only one percent of the information that passes into our consciousness will ever make it into the LTM (Tortora and Grabowski, 1993). Once information reaches the LTM it can be retained for an entire lifetime, although some pieces of information may decay over time with lack of use.

Research, particularly with patients suffering from brain damage, suggests strongly that there are different kinds of long-term memory. Squire (1992) divides long-term memory into procedural and declarative/propositional memory, with declarative memory holding two further sub-sections – episodic memory and semantic memory (Hayes, 2000). To obtain further information about the long-term memory, please refer to books listed in the reference section.

Influential Models of Memory

As research continues to unfold, we begin to appreciate just how complex and intricate the process of memory really is. Memory involves information being encoded, stored and then retrieved. In recent decades, psychologists and researchers have put forward various models that attempt to make sense of the mechanics of memory. Three of the most influential models are summarised below.

Two-Process Theory

Until the late 1950s research strongly favoured a unitary model of memory (Bourtchouladze, 2002), but by the 1960s, evidence began to accumulate for the division of memory into subsections (Gathercole, 1996). Numerous models acknowledged memory as a multi-system process, although it was the Atkinson and Shiffrin model (1968) that formalised the Two-Process Theory.

Atkinson and Shiffrin's Two-Process Theory is also referred to as the Modal Model and the Structural Model. The simplified diagram below outlines the essence of the model.

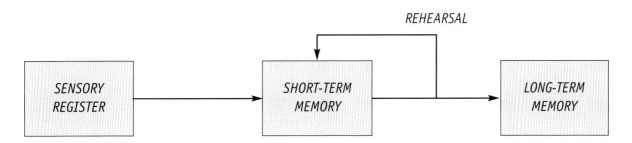

The model neatly organises memory into three distinct sub-sections. The sensory register absorbs incoming information and holds it for less than a second. A small percentage of that information will find its way into the STM. The transfer of information from the STM to the LTM requires rehearsal – this is one aspect of the model that has sparked huge discussion between researchers.

By the 1970s, the Two-Process Theory had become increasingly controversial. Research began to question the existence, and indeed the importance, of separate sub-sections. This shift in thought led to the Levels of Processing Theory.

Levels of Processing Theory

Craik and Lockhart (1972) argue that our ability to remember is influenced by the way in which we process information, rather than where we store it. They suggest that information that is of particular importance to us will be processed at a deeper cognitive level than information of less importance. The deeper the cognitive level at which information has been processed, the better its chances of being remembered. This model is neatly illustrated in Craik and Lockhart's study. Subjects were shown a list of words, and asked different types of questions relating to the words. One third of subjects were asked questions relating to the visual image of the words seen – for example 'Is it written in italics?', 'Is it in capital letters?' A third of subjects were asked questions relating to auditory aspects of the words – for example, whether the word rhymed with another word. The remaining third were asked questions relating to the semantic aspect of the words – for example, 'Would the word "log" fit into the sentence …?' (Hayes, 2000), or 'Is it a type of flower?' These three types of question involve different levels of processing.

Having answered the questions, subjects were then asked to recall the list of words. The study showed a clear difference in recall between the three subject groups. Subjects who were asked questions that prompted visual coding recalled the least amount of words. Those subjects who answered questions involving auditory coding recalled more than the first subject group, but significantly less than the third subject group, who used semantic coding. The study concluded that the deeper we process incoming information, the longer it will be remembered. The less attentive we are to incoming information, the less we process it and the quicker it is forgotten. However, the Levels of Processing theory is not without its critics, and research continues.

The Working Memory Model

The final model for discussion is that of Baddeley and Hitch (1974). The Working Memory Model provides a direct contrast to the STM store, as proposed in the Atkinson and Shiffrin model. Baddeley and Hitch argue 'that working memory is a complex, multi-component system rather than a single unitary store' (Cohen, Kiss & Le Voi, 1999). The Working Memory is believed to consist of the following systems:

1   Central Executive
2   Visuo-spatial sketch pad
3   Phonological loop
4   Acoustic store
5   Input register

Central Executive

Baddeley himself acknowledges that this system is the most 'complex and least understood component of the Working Model' (Gathercole, 1996). Briefly, the Central Executive is believed to be an active process, involved with cognitively demanding tasks. This system has limited storage capacity, and can only cope with small amounts of information at any one time. It is a system which is thought to be capable of monitoring and overseeing the other systems within working memory: all the other systems in the Working Memory Model are therefore commonly referred to as the 'slave' systems.

Visuo-Spatial Sketch Pad

This is a system that is believed to receive, store and manipulate non-verbal information, such as: colour, shape and appearance (visual features) and movement, speed, distance and positioning (spatial features) relating to objects and locations. The system is 'fired' by the Central Executive, as and when required.

Phonological Loop

This system is probably the most completely understood component of the model (Baddeley, 2001). Within this system there are two further components: the phonological store and the articulatory control. The phonological store is thought to be equipped to deal with the storing and manipulation of all speech-based information – information is believed to fade away within a period of approximately two seconds. The second component, the articulatory control, is responsible for sub-vocal articulatory rehearsal – the process in which information is rehearsed over and over again. As information begins to fade from the phonological store, memory traces can be strengthened and prolonged by pulling them from the articulatory control, and feeding them back into the phonological store. Current research data suggests that children do not tend to use sub-vocal rehearsal until the age of seven or eight years (Gathercole, 1996). (It should be noted that the phonological loop used to be known as the 'articulatory loop', and may be acknowledged as this in older research papers.)

Acoustic Store

This is where incoming acoustic information is coded.

Input Register

This system holds or represents the last word heard, acting almost like an 'inner ear'.

As with the first two models that we looked at, the Working Memory Model is not without its critics. It has been argued that the model is far too general, and fails to provide specific details about each component and the interaction between components.

Chapter 2
Strategies for Therapy

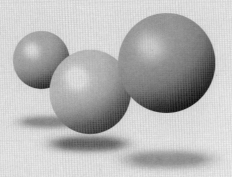

Characteristics of Children with Short-Term Memory Difficulties

Children with short-term memory difficulties may present with any number of the following characteristics:

1 Late referral to speech and language therapy services: referrals tend to be made by the child's educational placement, and there is often no previous history of speech and language difficulties.

2 Low self-confidence and limited self-esteem, particularly in relation to education and learning.

3 Passive nature within class activities.

4 Classwork not completed within given deadlines.

5 Poor academic progress: the child tends to struggle on a daily basis, across a range of subjects.

6 Strong long-term memory is often reported by parents and teachers.

7 Age-appropriate attention and listening skills.

8 Negative attitude towards, or perception of, school and/or teachers.

9 Heightened awareness of their own 'academic position' within the class – phrases such as 'I'm the thickest', or 'I can't do school' are not uncommon.

10 Difficulties in following verbal instructions.

11 Often hurry through memory tasks.

12 Score well below average on formal assessments of receptive language. Poor results may mislead one into believing that the child has delayed/disordered language skills. However, on closer examination, the child's errors tend to be sporadic and erratic, and do not highlight any specific linguistic weaknesses.

It is important to note that a number of these characteristics are also applicable across a range of client groups, such as those children with dyslexia, moderate learning difficulties and specific language impairment. For this reason alone, it is essential to confirm a diagnosis of STM difficulties, and formal and/or informal assessment will support this process. (See chapter 5 for a list of assessments.)

Intervention

For many children, particularly those between seven- and eleven-years-old, direct intervention can be of great benefit, and can have very positive results. As with all types of intervention however, the end result depends upon consistent carryover outside clinic sessions. The following list summarises the general benefits of intervention:

1   Progress is often evident within a relatively short period of time.
2   Short-term memory difficulties can often be resolved completely, leaving skills in line with the child's chronological age or general developmental level.
3   In some cases, short-term memory skills can exceed the child's chronological age/developmental level.
4   Progress appears to be long-term.
5   Improvements in short-term memory have a direct and positive impact on receptive language skills – the child is better equipped to retain specific pieces of incoming information, which allows him time for processing and then responding.
6   Confidence and self-esteem often develop during the sessions of intervention.
7   Older children tend to generalise memory strategies with ease.
8   Progress is seen within the classroom.

For those children whose progress appears to be extremely laboured, or perhaps even static, careful consideration needs to be given to the following points:

1   Does the child have access to regular and intensive practice of memory strategies outside the clinic session? Children require twice-daily practice. Do boundaries regarding carryover need to be re-addressed?

2   Is the child motivated to change? Is this the right time for the child to be receiving therapy? How comfortable with therapy is the child?

3   Are the memory tasks selected appropriate to the child's age, linguistic ability, and personal interests? Do you need to adapt the tasks to ensure that they are accessible to the child?

4   Is the child's memory level considerably weaker than his chronological and/or general developmental ability? Are your expected therapy outcomes reasonable?

5   Is this type of memory approach inappropriate for this particular child? Would this child perhaps benefit purely from memory aids? Or would he benefit from trying different strategies, such as naming, chunking, or grouping? (Please refer to page 14 for further information.)

Practical Ideas for Planning Individual Therapy

Please note that this programme of care has been designed for individual therapy. However, experienced clinicians may identify with certain aspects of this programme, and see the potential for group therapy: they are welcome to adapt the worksheets accordingly.

The Aim of Therapy
For the child to maximise his short-term memory, by acquiring and implementing memory strategies.

Therapy Objectives
1   For the child to have an understanding of 'memory'.
2   For the child to develop his knowledge of memory aids.
3   For the child to acquire, develop, and deploy memory strategies successfully.

4   For the child to maximise his memory capacity, through implementation of strategies.

5   To enhance the child's self-confidence and self-esteem.

Objective 1: Understanding Memory

It is important to ensure that children have a clear understanding of memory. Start by talking about the memory's function and use. Inform children of the general aims of therapy – these can often be established and/or amended in collaboration with older children.

Explore with the child factors that can weaken the performance of memory, such as medication, illness, tiredness, anxiety, hunger and environmental distractions. (When working with younger children, the word 'weak' can be replaced with 'sleepy'.) It is useful for children to know that everybody forgets things from time to time: a humorous account of when your memory last failed you can be very helpful at this stage.

Objective 2: Developing Knowledge of Memory Aids

Discuss and note down with the child items that can help to aid memory. Memory aids include calendars, diaries, pen and paper/notepad, pin boards, computer diaries and school planners. Good observation, listening and concentration skills, as well as the ability to ask others for help, will all assist the memory, and need to be discussed. The Matt Memory chart, in chapter 4 of this book, provides an alternative way for children to record the range of memory aids. Encourage children to use the memory aids most accessible to them, and monitor their use of these during the course of therapy: parents and/or teachers will need to be informed of the memory aids that the child wishes to use. Encourage children to think of family members, friends, or teachers who they have observed using memory aids recently.

Objective 3: Acquiring, Developing and Deploying Memory Strategies Successfully

Naming, rehearsal, visualisation, linking, chunking and grouping are all recognised strategies that can help to improve the performance of memory. For the majority of children, these (or at least some of these) strategies develop spontaneously, and are implemented without much thought. For a small number of children, however, memory strategies fail to develop naturally, and it is these children that can often benefit from specific teaching. This book focuses on two memory strategies: rehearsal and linking. (For those wishing to obtain further information on the remaining strategies, a comprehensive list of resources is provided in chapter 5.) The terms 'rehearsal' and 'linking' can often be too abstract for children, and for this reason have been re-termed 'repeating' and 'picturing' in this book, for the purpose of therapy.

Repeating Strategy

As the name now suggests, the repeating strategy involves receiving information, and sustaining it in the STM by repeating it over and over again – following Ebbinghaus' method (1885/1964). Repeating continues until the information is needed, so this strategy is only useful when remembering information for very short periods of time. When the attention is diverted or interrupted, repeating stops, and the information will fade from STM. You may be familiar with this strategy – for example, when you are looking up a telephone number in a phone directory, you are likely to keep the number 'alive' in STM by repeating it to yourself, until you have dialled successfully. Repeating is also very useful when entering sums on a calculator, or for remembering a verbal instruction.

Start by establishing the number of digits the child can hold consistently in his STM. Both informal and formal assessments can provide you with this information: the Informal Baseline test at the end of this chapter provides a method for determining a child's digit span, and chapter 5 contains a

STRATEGIES FOR THERAPY · 15

Table 1 *Normal Memory Development for Children in the General Population*

Age (in years)	Number of Digits held in STM
5.5	4
6	5
8.5	6
11–12	6–7

These figures represent the author's averaging of norms from a variety of sources.

comprehensive list of formal assessments. Table 1 shows perceived norms for memory development of children in the general population.

One would expect that a child of nine years of age could hold six digits in STM, for example. However, if the child can only remember three digits consistently, therapy would aim to build his digit span from three to four digits, and then from four digits to five, before developing to six digits. A child cannot be expected to progress straight from three digits to six digits: STM development needs to be gradual and sequential, and each step requires intensive practice.

Try to start and end repeating tasks on the number of digits that is comfortable for the child. For example, for the nine-year-old example above, therapy tasks would start at three digits, then build up to four digits, before ending back on three digits. This ensures that the child experiences success quickly at the start of a task, and then repeated success at the end.

When introducing children to the concept of repeating, start by modelling it yourself – for example '3649 ... 3649 ... 3649', then encourage the child to repeat with you, before prompting them to repeat alone. It is important that the child continues to repeat out loud during the development of their digit span: this allows the clinician to monitor and place any breakdown that occurs.

Children's difficulty in repetition tends to be consistent – for example, they may forget the last number in every set, or add an extra number to the digit sets. Having access to these periods of breakdown allows you to provide appropriate advice, guidance and management. Once the repeating strategy is established, the child should be encouraged to 'repeat quietly', or to 'repeat in your head', as it would be inappropriate for them to be repeating out loud beyond the context of the therapy sessions.

It is important to consider the potential difficulties for a child acquiring the repeating strategy. These include:

◻ Difficulty in progressing from one quantity of digits to the next.
Possible solution: If, as in the example above, a child succeeds at three digits, but has minimal or no success at four digits, you need to bridge this 'gap of demand'. Start by introducing four digit-sets in a pattern form:

1 alternating pattern: 1717, 2828, or 4343
2 paired pattern: 4422, 6611, or 5522
3 triple plus 1: 3331, 8889, or 7776

A pattern of numbers (1616) is much easier to remember than a random set of four numbers (1748). Once the child is proficient in recalling pattern sets, progress to random sets – ensuring that the random sets have the same number of digits as the pattern sets.

◻ Failure to recall the last digit in a set.
Possible solution: This problem may be caused by the child starting to repeat (sub-vocally) before having heard the whole set of digits. Ensure that the child continues to listen until the whole set of digits has been given.

Omitting a digit (in any position) may also indicate that the number of digits you are asking the child to remember is too great. In this case, you may need to move back to a pattern set.

▣ Inconsistency in the recall of numbers/words.
Possible solution: As children experience increasing success in recall, they sometimes attempt to bypass the repeating strategy altogether, thinking that they do not need it any more. It is important to address this issue immediately, and to help the child to understand that this is a life-long tool or 'magic trick' that they can continue to use when they are 10, 30, or 80 years old!

Chapter 3 provides a range of photocopiable worksheet tasks for clinic use, and for home/school carryover. The worksheets provide a varied and enjoyable way of practising and developing the child's confidence in using the repeating strategy for digits, words and sentences. The worksheets exercise the child's auditory STM (and, some would argue, the phonological loop of Baddeley and Hitch's Model – see chapter 1). Once the child has demonstrated an adequate command of the strategy, they should be encouraged to transfer the strategy into school lessons – for example, repeating sums while entering them on a calculator, or repeating an instruction – and for demands at home and/or in after-school clubs. Identify with the child (and, where possible, with parents and/or teachers) one or two specific activities within the child's natural environment where they can use the repeating strategy. Once the child is confident, and personal success develops, it is likely that the strategy will be generalised spontaneously.

The speed at which generalisation occurs varies from child to child, and according to the level of support received outside the clinic setting. For this reason, the process of generalisation should not be hurried. For some children, however, there may well be a continuing need for direct support from adults within the child's natural environment. It is worth mentioning here how important it is that parents and teachers (including Advanced/General Teaching Assistants) are made fully aware of the child's memory strategy, and have an appreciation of the rationale behind it. It is also important to ensure that the child's parents and teachers have a clear understanding of the terms short-term and long-term memory – do not assume that everybody knows this: they don't!

Picturing Strategy

This strategy can help children to retain information for longer periods of time, and is a little more robust than repeating. It is interesting to note that children often report that they prefer the repeating strategy, despite having greater success with the picturing strategy during recall. When introducing the picturing strategy, it may be useful to explain the mechanics of picturing with the idea of all of us having a 'camera' in our heads – a camera that can take photographs and provide picture-like images.

In order to help to familiarise the child with their 'internal camera', start by asking the child to think about their last school trip, bedroom, favourite car, or something similar. This will help to fire their own internal images/pictures on that subject. It should be noted that the visual image of recall, in this case, is from the child's long-term, rather than short-term, memory: however, it is still a useful exercise, and provides the child with the opportunity to understand and explore the 'internal camera'. Children sometimes need to be reassured that their internal pictures are not 'picture-book clear' – indeed, faded images are perfectly normal, and strong enough to work from. Another useful introduction to internal visual images is to show the child an unfamiliar object for a few seconds, then remove it from view. The child then has to describe what they have just seen, using their internal image/picture (memory), part of the visuo-spatial sketch pad of the Baddeley and Hitch model, described in chapter 1.

Building from here, the aim of picturing is to develop the ability to remember a series of items, by creating a short story – a story that incorporates the objects in sequential order. In creating a story, semantic connections are fired, and visual images produced. What once started out as a series of random objects now becomes a meaningful story. This memory strategy reflects the work of Craik and Lockhart, who concluded that the more meaningful the stimulus, the deeper we process it, and the better our chances of recalling it. Clinicians will need to start by showing the child some random objects from around the clinic room. Place the objects in a line on the table, directly in front of the child. The number of objects tends to be the child's digit span ability plus one, so, if you are working with a child who has a digit span of three, you need to present them with four objects. Work with the child to create a story that incorporates each object. Ensure that the story makes a direct reference to each object, and that there is a meaningful link between them. Explain to the child that the memory loves unusual and funny details, and that these should be included wherever possible.

Help the child to practise saying the story out loud. It does not have to be word perfect, but does need to include the general content and sequential order of objects. Then ask the child to turn away from the objects. At this point you are ready for the child to use the story/picture in his head to help him recall each object. Ask the child to go through the story in his head, and to shout out only the objects that needed to be remembered as they occur in the story. This activity will help to develop visuo-spatial memory.

As with the repeating strategy, children should be encouraged to create their stories aloud during clinic sessions. This allows clinicians to guide a child, if breakdown occurs while using this strategy. Increase the number of objects as the child becomes proficient. A number of photocopiable worksheets are provided within this resource. The worksheets provide a safe and controlled context in which children can practise and develop their second strategy.

Informal Baseline Test for Therapy

Introduction

You will need

Pen or pencil

Photocopy of the test sheet

How to administer

This test provides a quick, informal assessment, which can be used at the beginning and end of therapy, and after a period of consolidation following therapy intervention.

Begin the test by asking the child to turn away from you: this minimises distraction, and ensures that the test is a test of auditory memory. Explain to the child that you are going to begin by reading out some numbers, and that you would like him to repeat them back to you, in the same order. As you read out each set of numbers on the test sheet, ensure that you maintain a steady pace of speech, and do not chunk the numbers together. Allow the child plenty of time to respond.

As in any test situation, children can become quite anxious when they know that repetition of a test item is not allowed. For this reason, test items should be repeated at the child's request. However, if repetition is needed, the test item is automatically recorded as a fail, although the child should not be made aware of this. The test is to be administered in its entirety. Correct responses score 1 point. Incorrect responses, including responses that have the appropriate numbers but incorrect sequence, score 0. Where repetition of a test item is required, this also scores 0, even if the child's second response is correct. For no response score 0. Note the total score in the space provided. The test data should establish the child's maximum digit span – the last digit span subsection that elicits four correct responses. Compare this information with the 'norms' given in Table 1 of this chapter to establish whether intervention is appropriate. Please note that this is an informal screening test, and should not be viewed as an alternative to published, standardised assessments.

Informal Baseline Test

Record Sheet

Child's name _____

Date of Baseline Test _____   Child's age _____

Date of Retest _____   Child's age _____

DIGIT SPAN						BASELINE	RETEST
				5	7	☐	☐
				9	2	☐	☐
				0	4	☐	☐
				6	1	☐	☐
			8	5	2	☐	☐
			2	5	1	☐	☐
			9	3	8	☐	☐
			0	7	3	☐	☐
		4	9	0	2	☐	☐
		6	2	7	1	☐	☐
		1	8	3	5	☐	☐
		2	7	1	9	☐	☐
	8	0	2	5	7	☐	☐
	6	4	1	7	3	☐	☐
	5	3	0	1	4	☐	☐
	7	2	5	7	3	☐	☐
9	7	1	3	5	2	☐	☐
2	0	4	6	9	3	☐	☐
7	3	2	5	0	1	☐	☐
6	8	1	3	8	4	☐	☐

Baseline Score ____ 20   Retest Score ____ 20

Chapter 3
Memory activities for therapy and practice

Guidelines for Using Memory Tasks

◻ This resource is primarily designed for individual therapy programmes, but clinicians may wish to adapt some of the tasks for group therapy sessions.

◻ Children should be introduced to the repeating and picturing strategies *before* worksheets are handed out.

◻ Do not introduce the repeating and picturing strategies together. Ensure that the child has an understanding of, and is developing competence in, one strategy before introducing the second.

◻ Worksheets and instructions are photocopiable.

◻ Children are not expected to complete every single worksheet. The games should be selected according to the child's age, linguistic ability, level of learning, interests, and the strategy to be practised, and do not need to be administered in the order in which they are presented.

◻ Worksheets are suitable for both clinic sessions and as homework. Daily practice is paramount in helping children to reach their optimum level. Children must practise their digit-span development at least twice a day.

◻ The worksheets have been designed to be easy to use and quick to score. Clinicians are encouraged to adjust the demands and/or delivery of a task where necessary: it is better to re-shape a task to suit a child's needs rather than shaping the child to fit the task!

▣ It is often useful to encourage children to take a turn at being the 'director' in tasks. This not only removes demands for a short period, but also provides children with an opportunity to observe someone else implementing memory strategies and aids. Clinicians may wish to stop repeating halfway through a task, be distracted by an environmental noise, or perhaps fidget while being given a task instruction. The child can then have an opportunity to identify why the clinician's memory may have failed in a particular task. This is a very effective way of developing children's self-monitoring and self-awareness skills – and they enjoy telling a clinician where she has gone wrong!

▣ Each task consists of a series of exercises at graded levels. If a child requires further practice at a specific level, clinicians are encouraged to expand from the worksheets. Readjust the tasks' total scores accordingly.

▣ It should be noted that chapter 4 provides a selection of progress charts, recording forms and scenarios. These can be used in sessions by the children themselves to record their development. The Memory Chart is particularly useful for encouraging children to reflect on tasks they have completed successfully.

▣ The tasks provide a structured and enjoyable environment for children to acquire and reinforce memory strategies. As with all types of intervention, praise and reassurance is vital in building a child's motivation, confidence and ability.

▣ This book does not claim to be the ultimate package of care for children with short-term memory difficulties. Nevertheless, it is hoped that the worksheets will provide a varied accompaniment to current resources, or, at the very least, provide the foundations for further resources ideas.

Introductory Picturing Game

You will need

Photocopies of the 'Introductory Picturing Game' worksheets

How to play

Help the child to link the pictures together to form a picture story in his mind. When all of the pictures have been linked together, turn the worksheet over. Encourage the child to re-tell the story, aloud. Then ask the child to re-tell the story again, but silently to themselves, telling you the target pictures as they crop up in their picture story.

Introductory Picturing Game *(continued)*

Child's name _____ Date _____

Game 1

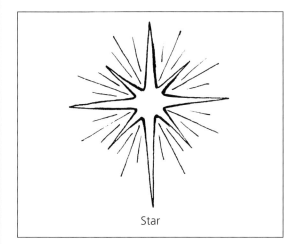

Star

Boy

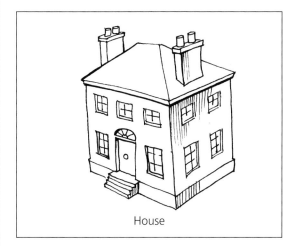

House

Flower

Cloud

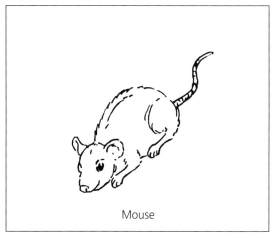

Mouse

Total Remembered _____/6

Introductory Picturing Game *(continued)*

Child's name _____ Date _____

Game 2

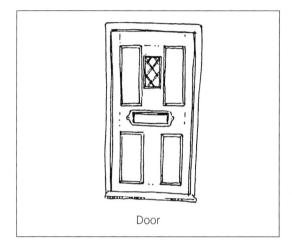

Door

Sun

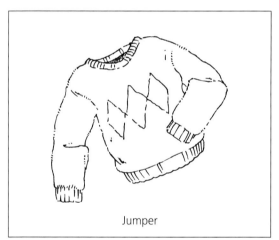

Jumper

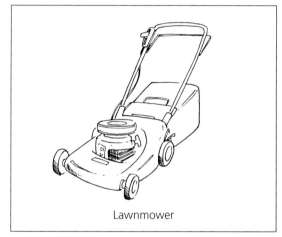

Lawnmower

Bottles

Tap

Total Remembered _____/6

PICTURING

WORKSHEET 1

Introductory Picturing Game *(continued)*

Child's name _____ Date _____

Game 3

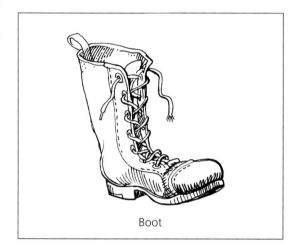

Boot

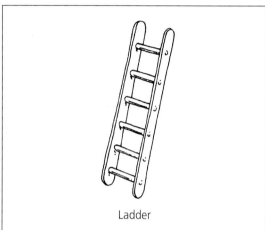

Ladder

Chimney

Cup

Cloud

Chair

Total Remembered _____/6

Introductory Picturing Game *(continued)*

Child's name _____ Date _____

Game 4

Boy

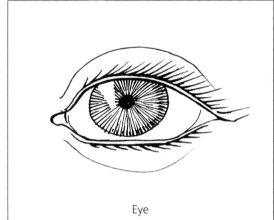

Eye

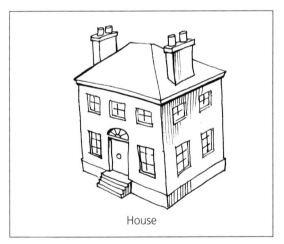

House

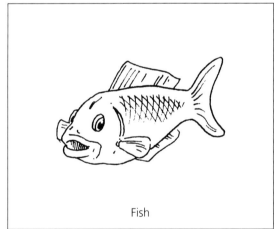

Fish

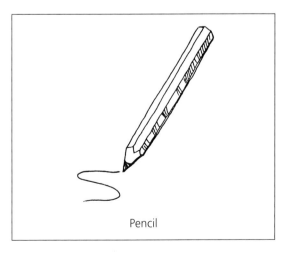

Pencil

Duck

Total Remembered _____/6

Introductory Picturing Game (continued)

Child's name _____ Date _____

Game 5

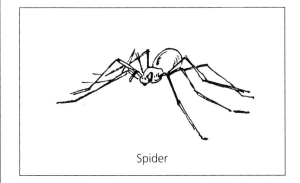

Spider

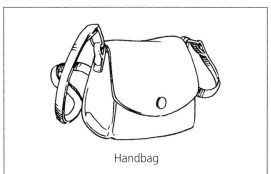

Handbag

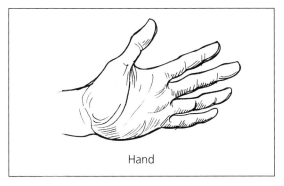

Hand

Candle

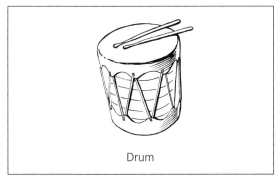

Drum

Cat

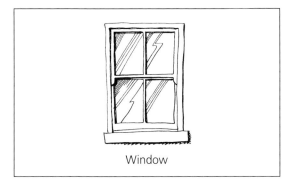

Window

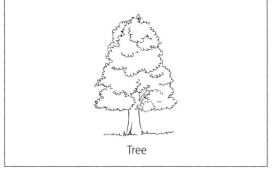

Tree

Total Remembered _____/8

Introductory Picturing Game *(continued)*

Child's name _____ Date _____

Game 6

Tent

Girl

Clock

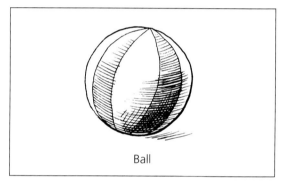
Ball

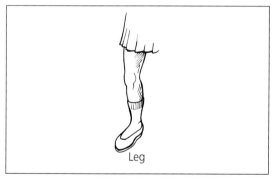
Leg

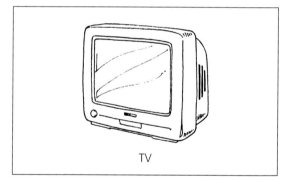
TV

Sofa/Settee

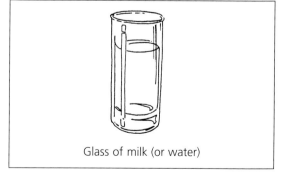
Glass of milk (or water)

Total Remembered _____/8

Introductory Picturing Game *(continued)*

Child's name _____ Date _____

Game 7

Telephone

Radio

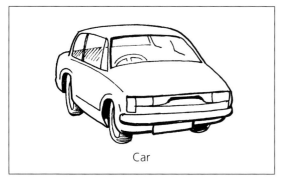
Car

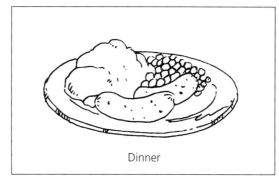
Dinner

Book

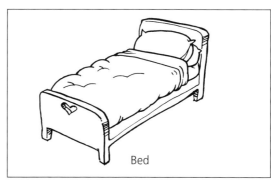
Bed

Ghost

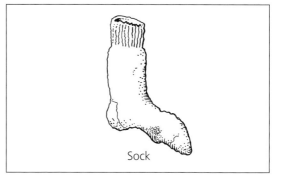
Sock

Total Remembered _____/8

Storytelling

You will need

Photocopies of the 'Storytelling' worksheets

How to play

Help the child to link the words together to form a visual story in his mind for each game. You may need to read the words out loud for the child. Where necessary, write the child's story in the space provided below the list of words, highlighting the target words to be remembered. Now remove the worksheet from the child's sight and see how much of the story he can remember. Next, encourage the child to retell his visual story silently to himself, but to shout out the key words as they crop up. Score as appropriate.

Storytelling *(continued)*

Child's name _____ Date _____

Game 1

cup　　　**coat**　　　**sun**　　　**grass**　　　**mouse**　　　**water**

_____

_____

_____

_____

_____

_____

_____

_____

_____

_____

_____

_____

Total Remembered _____/6

PICTURING

Storytelling *(continued)*

Child's name _____ Date _____

WORKSHEET 2

Game 2

horse	boat	glass	nurse	bed	car

_____

_____

_____

_____

_____

_____

_____

_____

_____

_____

_____

_____

_____

Total Remembered _____/6

Storytelling *(continued)*

Child's name _____ Date _____

Game 3

rainbow   **shoe**   **milk**   **ball**   **sea**   **road**

_____

_____

_____

_____

_____

_____

_____

_____

_____

_____

_____

_____

Total Remembered _____/6

Storytelling *(continued)*

PICTURING

WORKSHEET 2

Child's name _____ Date _____

Game 4

tractor	bus	star	tree	clock	snake

_____

_____

_____

_____

_____

_____

_____

_____

_____

_____

_____

_____

Total Remembered _____/6

Storytelling *(continued)*

Child's name _____ Date _____

Game 5

    sea   **rain**   **shop**   **hat**   **train**   **puddle**

_____

_____

_____

_____

_____

_____

_____

_____

_____

_____

_____

_____

Total Remembered _____/6

PICTURING

WORKSHEET 2

Storytelling *(continued)*

Child's name _____ Date _____

Game 6

castle   **coat**   **hammer**   **ice**   **man**   **bottle**

_____

_____

_____

_____

_____

_____

_____

_____

_____

_____

_____

_____

_____

_____

_____

_____

Total Remembered _____/6

Storytelling *(continued)*

PICTURING

WORKSHEET 2

Child's name _____ Date _____

Game 7

wheel	baby	window	phone	button	door

_____

_____

_____

_____

_____

_____

_____

_____

_____

_____

_____

Total Remembered _____/6

Telephone Numbers

You will need

Paper and a pen or pencil.

Photocopies of the child's recording sheet and the page of telephone numbers

How to play

The adult reads out the list of telephone numbers and encourages the child to repeat each set of numbers. Pace the exercise to the child's speed and ensure you do not 'chunk' the numbers when reading them aloud, eg, '7 … 8 … 6 … 2 …', and not '78 … 62 … 1'.

You can increase the difficulty of this game by asking children to respond by:

▣ entering the numbers on a calculator;

▣ dialling the numbers on a toy telephone;

▣ writing the numbers down on the recording sheet provided.

Rather than just repeating the numbers back to you, these options provide a time-delay, and demand use of the repeating strategy to counteract this.

List of telephone numbers

Introduction: three digits		*Basic: four digits*	
a	217	a	1250
b	618	b	1789
c	437	c	3201
d	972	d	1751
e	813	e	2483
f	574	f	9136
g	178	g	6295
h	659	h	4281
i	461	i	5720
j	152	j	3816

Telephone Numbers *(continued)*

REPEATING

WORKSHEET 3

Medium: five digits

a 78621
b 63120
c 90545
d 23968
e 41517
f 97234
g 76953
h 20578
i 61439
j 14037

Hard: six digits

a 241868
b 256883
c 229440
d 552471
e 439459
f 981571
g 349728
h 187401
i 262801
j 810439

If a child has difficulty moving from one set of digits to another – for example the child can consistently recall three digits, but is unable to recall four digits – bridge this transition by making up four digit phone numbers that have a pattern, such as 2233, 6611, 4141, 8383, 7772, 6665. Once the pattern sets are achieved consistently, the child is then ready for the four mixed digits again. (See the 'Repeating Strategy' section of chapter 2 for specific guidance.)

Telephone Numbers *(continued)*

Recording sheet

Child's name _____ Date _____

Number of digits to recall _____

a _____

b _____

c _____

d _____

e _____

f _____

g _____

h _____

i _____

j _____

Total Correct _____/10

Colouring Game

You will need

Coloured pens/pencils

Instruction sheets

Photocopies of colour grid sheet

How to play

Give the child a copy of the colour grid. Select the appropriate instruction level for the child's ability. Read out each set of colours, pausing between sets to allow time to respond. The child will respond by colouring in each set of colours on the grid provided.

The child should listen to the full instruction before selecting the coloured pens or pencils required. These should be selected and used in the order that they occur. Explain to the child that a colour may occur twice within the same grid.

Photocopy additional colour grid pages if the child requires further reinforcement at a particular level, and devise your own colour combinations (or you could read the colour sets backwards).

Colouring Game *(continued)*

Instruction sheet

Child's name _____ Date _____

Level 1 (Three pieces of information)

				Score (✓ or ✗)
1	Red	Blue	Green	☐
2	Black	Pink	Blue	☐
3	Green	Blue	Red	☐
4	Orange	Grey	Black	☐
5	Yellow	Red	Blue	☐
6	Black	Blue	Brown	☐
7	Red	Pink	Yellow	☐
8	Yellow	Pink	Blue	☐
9	Black	Green	Red	☐
10	Green	Red	Orange	☐
11	Red	Blue	Yellow	☐
12	Orange	Black	Yellow	☐
13	Yellow	Pink	Red	☐
14	Brown	Yellow	Blue	☐
15	Blue	Red	Green	☐

Total _____/15

Colouring Game *(continued)*

Instruction sheet

Child's name _____ Date _____

REPEATING

WORKSHEET 4

Level 2 (Four pieces of information)

					Score (✓ or ✗)
1	Black	Red	Blue	Green	☐
2	Red	Orange	Blue	Black	☐
3	Yellow	Green	Red	Black	☐
4	Orange	Yellow	Green	Brown	☐
5	Blue	Black	Red	Yellow	☐
6	Grey	Black	Green	Blue	☐
7	Red	Yellow	Blue	Blue	☐
8	Yellow	Green	Brown	Yellow	☐
9	Blue	Orange	Green	Red	☐
10	Red	Pink	Yellow	Blue	☐
11	Pink	Pink	Red	Blue	☐
12	Brown	Red	Black	Yellow	☐
13	Orange	Blue	Grey	Red	☐
14	Black	Brown	Grey	Grey	☐
15	Pink	Yellow	Green	Blue	☐

Total _____ /15

Colouring Game *(continued)*

Instruction sheet

Child's name _____ Date _____

Level 3 (Five pieces of information)

						Score (✓ or ✗)
1	Blue	Black	Red	Blue	Yellow	☐
2	Red	Yellow	Black	Grey	Blue	☐
3	Red	Red	Blue	Green	Pink	☐
4	Green	Black	Grey	Red	Blue	☐
5	Blue	Green	Blue	Green	Red	☐
6	Black	Red	Yellow	Green	Blue	☐
7	Yellow	Red	Red	Green	Green	☐
8	Red	Pink	Grey	Blue	Brown	☐
9	Pink	Grey	Blue	Yellow	Red	☐
10	Blue	Red	Yellow	Green	Brown	☐
11	Green	Blue	Green	Red	Grey	☐
12	Brown	Grey	Black	Orange	Black	☐
13	Grey	Yellow	Red	Yellow	Grey	☐
14	Yellow	Blue	Orange	Red	Black	☐
15	Black	Green	Grey	Blue	Red	☐

Total _____/15

Colouring Game *(continued)*

Colour Grids

Child's name _____ Date _____ Level _____

Answer 1

Answer 2

Answer 3

Answer 4

Answer 5

Answer 6

Answer 7

Answer 8

Answer 9

Answer 10

Answer 11

Answer 12

Answer 13

Answer 14

Answer 15

Action Game

You will need

Floor space

A pen and the instruction sheets

How to play:

Read out each command. Encourage the child to listen and respond by carrying out the action. The child should be standing in a clear space for this game. The child's responses can be recorded on the instruction sheets provided.

NB Some commands are open to interpretation – score responses accordingly.

Action Game *(continued)*

Instruction sheet

Child's name _____ Date _____

Level 1

Can you: ● Score (✓ or ✗)

1 Clap? ☐

2 Hop? ☐

3 Wave? ☐

4 Turn around? ☐

5 Jump? ☐

6 Cough? ☐ Total _____/6

Level 2

Can you: Score (✓ or ✗)

1 Stamp your feet? ☐

2 Wave your hand slowly? ☐

3 Turn around quickly? ☐

4 Wiggle your thumbs? ☐

5 Pat your head? ☐

6 Sit down and smile? ☐

7 Walk and wave? ☐ Total _____/7

REPEATING

WORKSHEET 5

Action Game *(continued)*

Child's name _____ Date _____

Level 3   Score
Can you: (✓ or ✗)

  1 Jump forwards, and say 'hello'?   ☐

  2 Hop backwards, and then sit down?   ☐

  3 Pat your tummy, and stick your tongue out?   ☐

  4 Sit down, fold your arms, and smile?   ☐

  5 Run, and touch the door?   ☐

  6 Cough loudly, and then hop?   ☐

  7 Point to the door and the floor?   ☐

  8 Skip to the table, and then sit down?   ☐

  9 Pat your tummy and your head?   ☐ Total _____/9

Level 4   Score
Can you: (✓ or ✗)

  1 Lie down, cross your arms, and smile?   ☐

  2 Walk to the window, then jump to a chair?   ☐

  3 Wiggle your fingers, and close your eyes?   ☐

  4 Put your hands on your back, and tap your fingers?   ☐

  5 Count to five, and jump backwards?   ☐

  6 Turn around, walk backwards, and clap loudly?   ☐

  7 Look up, point to the sky, and then wave?   ☐

  8 Hold your ears, and walk backwards slowly?   ☐ Total _____/8

Chinese Whispers – Almost!

You will need

A minimum of four people

Pen and paper

Photocopy of the recording chart and 'digit levels' sheet

How to play

Ask the children/family members to sit in a line – this prevents lip reading! Choose the appropriate task level for the game. Explain to the players that you will be the chief and will whisper one set of digits to the person at the end of the line. The information will then be whispered from person to person until it reaches the other end of the line. The last person in the line will then write the numbers down and read them back to the chief. If the set of numbers is read back correctly, the players have won two points. If the numbers are incorrect, the chief wins two points. Record the points on the chart.

Chinese Whispers – Almost! *(continued)*

Recording Chart

Level _____

	Chief	v	Team
Set A	_____		_____
Set B	_____		_____
Set C	_____		_____
Set D	_____		_____
Set E	_____		_____
Set F	_____		_____
Set G	_____		_____

Total points _____   Total points _____

Chinese Whispers – Almost! *(continued)*

Digit Levels

Level 1 **(Two digits)**	**Level 2** **(Three digits)**	**Level 3** **(Four digits)**
a 0 7	**a** 0 1 6	**a** 2 1 3 4
b 3 1	**b** 2 4 3	**b** 5 8 1 0
c 4 8	**c** 0 7 4	**c** 9 3 6 1
d 6 2	**d** 5 9 3	**d** 7 4 1 2
e 1 6	**e** 8 2 1	**e** 0 8 2 5
f 3 8	**f** 5 4 1	**f** 3 7 9 4
g 4 2	**g** 8 6 5	**g** 1 2 5 3

If children fail at Level 3, present them with four-digit patterns – for example, 1 1 2 2, 4 4 6 6, 1 6 1 6, 2 8 2 8 – before working up to four random digits.

Level 4 **(Five digits)**	**Level 5** **(Six digits)**
a 2 4 8 1 6	**a** 2 4 8 3 4 1
b 3 4 2 0 1	**b** 3 2 6 6 4 5
c 7 5 3 2 3	**c** 7 2 8 1 3 5
d 9 0 7 4 5	**d** 9 3 0 2 8 8
e 1 6 2 5 7	**e** 6 1 1 9 5 2
f 9 1 5 3 9	**f** 2 4 5 8 7 0
g 8 2 4 6 3	**g** 5 8 4 1 6 9

If children fail at Level 4, present them with five-digit patterns – for example, 2 1 2 1 2, 7 4 7 4 7, 1 1 3 3 5, 4 4 1 1 9 – before working up to the five random digits above.

If children fail at Level 5, present them with six-digit patterns – for example, 2 2 3 3 4 4, 7 7 8 8 1 1, 6 2 6 2 4 4 – before moving on to the six random digits.

Bingo!

You will need

Coloured pen or pencil

The bingo caller's number sheet

Photocopies of bingo card sheets

How to play

The adult acts as the bingo caller, and reads out the appropriate level of digits from the bingo caller's number sheet. The child should listen to the numbers, then mark them off on the bingo card in the same order as they are read out. Ensure that the child does not mark off the numbers until he has heard the complete number set. The child's score can be recorded on the bingo caller's number sheet or on the bingo cards.

Younger children enjoy this game more when the adult adopts a bingo caller's voice!

Bingo! *(continued)*

Bingo Caller's Numbers

Three Digits				Score (✓ or ✗)	
a	5	2	7	☐	
b	7	2	3	☐	
c	4	1	9	☐	
d	8	1	4	☐	
e	2	1	6	☐	Total _____/5

Four Digits					Score (✓ or ✗)	
a	7	0	3	2	☐	
b	9	2	7	1	☐	
c	8	1	6	4	☐	
d	0	4	4	2	☐	
e	5	7	1	6	☐	
f	1	2	3	7	☐	
g	3	1	8	2	☐	
h	7	4	5	8	☐	
i	8	1	6	4	☐	
j	8	2	5	6	☐	
k	4	6	2	8	☐	
l	0	7	3	5	☐	
m	6	2	3	1	☐	
n	6	9	2	1	☐	
o	3	5	1	7	☐	Total _____/15

Bingo! *(continued)*

Bingo Caller's Numbers

Five Digits   Score (✓ or ✗)

a 7 3 9 5 2 ☐

b 9 5 7 2 3 ☐

c 1 0 3 8 4 ☐

d 1 2 3 6 5 ☐

e 3 7 5 0 7 ☐

f 2 5 1 8 3 ☐

g 2 4 1 5 6 ☐

h 6 1 2 5 4 ☐

i 1 8 6 0 5 ☐

j 8 5 3 9 1 ☐

k 8 4 4 3 6 ☐

l 0 1 8 2 0 ☐

m 8 4 5 1 6 ☐

n 2 6 1 0 8 ☐

o 3 8 1 7 1 ☐   Total _____/15

Bingo! *(continued)*

Bingo Caller's Numbers

Six Digits   Score (✓ or ✗)

a	5	1	8	3	0	2	☐
b	4	1	7	8	3	2	☐
c	7	0	3	1	4	1	☐
d	8	7	5	1	6	2	☐
e	3	2	7	8	5	1	☐
f	9	8	1	7	4	3	☐
g	3	0	5	6	9	1	☐
h	7	4	3	1	1	2	☐
i	0	3	9	5	2	1	☐
j	6	4	7	3	2	0	☐
k	7	8	1	3	4	2	☐
l	0	6	0	4	5	7	☐
m	5	1	0	8	1	4	☐
n	5	3	8	4	1	6	☐
o	7	3	9	0	4	6	☐

Total _____/15

REPEATING

WORKSHEET 7

Bingo! *(continued)*

Bingo Cards: Three Digits

Child's name _____ Date _____

a

5	7
0	2

Score _____/3

b

3	2
7	1

Score _____/3

c

6	9
1	4

Score _____/3

d

2	8
4	1

Score _____/3

e

6	2
1	7

Score _____/3

Bingo! *(continued)*

Bingo Cards: Four Digits

Child's name _____ Date _____

a

2	7	3
4	0	1

Score _____/4

b

1	3	9
7	4	2

Score _____/4

c

5	4	1
6	8	2

Score _____/4

d

5	2	0
7	4	4

Score _____/4

e

1	8	7
6	5	2

Score _____/4

f

2	8	7
3	0	1

Score _____/4

g

6	8	3
1	5	2

Score _____/4

h

7	2	1
5	8	4

Score _____/4

Bingo! *(continued)*

Bingo! *(continued)*

Bingo Cards: Four Digits

Child's name _____ Date _____

i

2	8	1
6	4	3

Score _____/4

j

3	6	1
5	2	8

Score _____/4

k

2	7	3
4	6	8

Score _____/4

l

0	5	9
3	1	7

Score _____/4

m

2	5	6
7	3	1

Score _____/4

n

2	0	1
6	9	8

Score _____/4

o

7	1	5
4	3	2

Score _____/4

Bingo! *(continued)*

Bingo Cards: Five Digits

REPEATING

WORKSHEET 7

Child's name _____ Date _____

a

7	1	0	5
2	8	3	9

Score _____/5

b

2	1	0	5
7	9	3	4

Score _____/5

c

5	8	2	7
1	4	0	3

Score _____/5

d

7	8	1	3
5	6	2	0

Score _____/5

e

1	0	5	9
7	7	4	3

Score _____/5

f

6	1	5	2
3	8	7	9

Score _____/5

g

7	8	2	1
6	5	3	4

Score _____/5

h

5	6	3	0
1	4	8	2

Score _____/5

Bingo! *(continued)*

Bingo Cards: Five Digits

Child's name _____ Date _____

i

5	2	1	4
6	3	8	0

Score _____/5

j

2	1	0	5
8	3	9	2

Score _____/5

k

2	5	4	4
6	8	0	3

Score _____/5

l

2	7	5	0
8	3	1	0

Score _____/5

m

6	2	1	5
3	4	8	0

Score _____/5

n

2	1	5	8
7	0	6	4

Score _____/5

o

1	2	8	1
6	4	3	7

Score _____/5

Bingo! *(continued)*

Bingo Cards: Six Digits

Child's name _____ Date _____

a

6	4	1	0
3	5	8	2

Score _____/6

b

0	9	3	8
2	1	4	7

Score _____/6

c

2	1	0	8
4	3	1	7

Score _____/6

d

2	8	0	5
6	7	1	4

Score _____/6

e

9	3	0	7
5	2	1	8

Score _____/6

f

2	0	8	4
3	9	1	7

Score _____/6

g

2	5	7	6
3	0	9	1

Score _____/6

h

7	0	8	1
2	4	3	1

Score _____/6

Bingo! *(continued)*

Bingo Cards: Six Digits

Child's name _____ Date _____

i

7	1	0	5
2	8	3	9

Score _____/6

j

2	4	1	3
6	8	7	0

Score _____/6

k

2	8	1	0
7	4	3	5

Score _____/6

l

7	0	1	6
5	4	3	0

Score _____/6

m

1	8	7	3
4	5	1	0

Score _____/6

n

3	8	1	5
4	2	6	0

Score _____/6

o

5	4	3	7
6	9	0	1

Score _____/6

Shape Tank

You will need

Photocopies of the tank sheet and shapes sheet

Scissors and the instruction sheet

How to play

Note: The child must have knowledge of left/right and shapes for this game.

Cut out the range of shapes from the shape sheet and place them in front of the child, along with the tank sheet. Ensure that the rectangle shapes are placed on end at the start of each game, thus:

Select the appropriate task level. Read out the instructions slowly for each task, and allow the child time to respond to each instruction. The child must select the shapes in the order they are given. When you have delivered all the instructions per game, show your tank to the child to see if the child's tank matches yours. Adjust the task level according to the child's ability. The child's responses can be recorded on the instruction sheet.

Shape Tank *(continued)*

Shapes sheet

Cut out the shapes before starting the game.

Shape Tank *(continued)*

Tank sheet

REPEATING

WORKSHEET 8

LEFT	RIGHT

Remove the shapes after each game.

Shape Tank *(continued)*

Instruction sheet – Level 1

Game 1

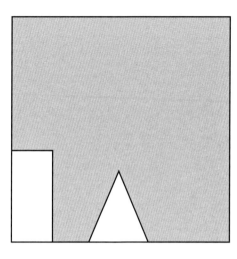

Instructions   Score (✓ or ✗)

a   Select a rectangle and a triangle.   ☐

b   Put the triangle in the centre of the floor of your tank.   ☐

c   Put the rectangle in the bottom left-hand corner.   ☐

                                                    Total _____/3

Game 2

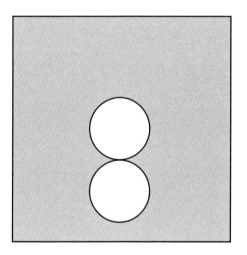

Instructions   Score (✓ or ✗)

a   Select two circles.   ☐

b   Place one circle in the centre of the tank.   ☐

c   Place the other circle under the first circle.   ☐

                                                    Total _____/3

Shape Tank *(continued)*

Instruction sheet – Level 1

Game 3

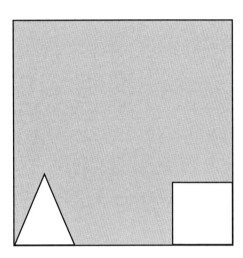

Instructions	Score (✓ or ✗)
a Select a square and a triangle.	☐
b Put the square in the bottom right-hand corner of the tank.	☐
c Place the triangle in the bottom left-hand corner of the tank.	☐

Total _____/3

Make up some more instructions if the child requires further practice at this level.

Shape Tank *(continued)*

Instruction sheet – Level 2

Game 1

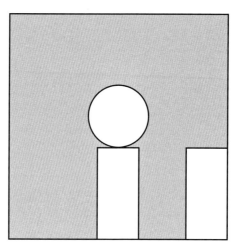

Instructions

Score (✓ or ✗)

a   Select two rectangles and a circle.   ☐

b   Place one rectangle at the bottom of the tank in the middle.   ☐

c   Place other rectangle at the bottom right-hand corner.   ☐

d   Place the circle on top of the rectangle in the middle of the tank.   ☐

Total _____/4

Shape Tank *(continued)*

Instruction sheet – Level 2

Game 2

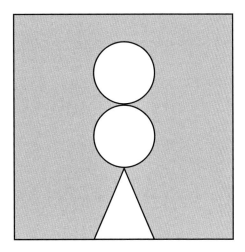

Instructions   Score (✓ or ✗)

a   Select two circles and a triangle.

b   Put the triangle in the middle of the floor of the tank.

c   Put a circle on top of the triangle.

d   Put the other circle on top of the first circle.

Total _____/4

REPEATING

WORKSHEET 8

Shape Tank *(continued)*

Instruction sheet – Level 2

REPEATING

WORKSHEET 8

Game 3

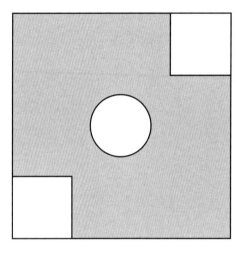

Instructions   Score (✓ or ✗)

a   Select two squares and a circle.

b   Put one square at the top right-hand corner of
        the tank.

c   Put the other square in the bottom left-hand corner.

d   Put the circle between the squares, in the centre of
        the tank.

Total _____/4

Shape Tank *(continued)*

Instruction sheet – Level 3

Game 1

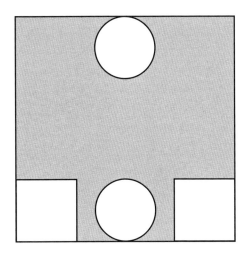

Instructions   Score (✓ or ✗)

a   Select two circles and two squares.   ☐

b   Place one circle in the centre at the top of the tank.   ☐

c   Place the other circle at the bottom of the tank,
        below the first circle.   ☐

d   Put a square in both bottom corners of the tank.   ☐

                                                    Total _____/4

Shape Tank *(continued)*

Instruction sheet – Level 3

Game 2

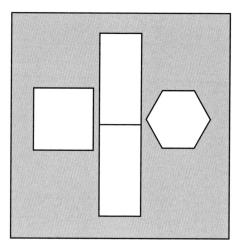

Instructions

Score (✓ or ✗)

a Select two rectangles, a square and a hexagon.

☐

b Stand the rectangles on top of each other in the middle of the tank.

☐

c Place the hexagon in the middle of the space on the right.

☐

d Place the square in the middle of the space on the left.

☐

Total _____/4

REPEATING

WORKSHEET 8

Shape Tank *(continued)*
Instruction sheet – Level 3

Game 3

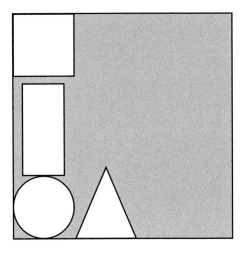

Instructions   Score (✓ or ✗)

a   Select a circle, a rectangle, a triangle and a square.   ☐

b   Place the circle in the bottom left-hand corner of
the tank.   ☐

c   Place a rectangle above and a triangle next to
the circle.   ☐

d   Place the square in the top left-hand corner.   ☐

Total _____/4

REPEATING

WORKSHEET 8

Shape Tank *(continued)*

Instruction sheet – Level 4

Game 1

Instructions	Score (✓ or ✗)
a Select two triangles, two circles and a rectangle.	☐
b Place the two triangles in the centre of the floor of the tank.	☐
c Turn the rectangle on its side and place it on top of the two triangles.	☐
d Place the two circles on top of the rectangle, one at either end.	☐

Total _____/4

Shape Tank *(continued)*

Instruction sheet – Level 4

Game 2

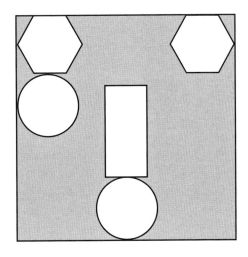

Instructions

Score (✓ or ✗)

a Select a rectangle, two circles and two hexagons. ☐

b Place a circle in the middle of the floor of the tank, and then a rectangle on top of it. ☐

c Place one hexagon in the top right-hand corner of the tank. ☐

d Place the remaining hexagon in the remaining top corner, and the circle below it. ☐

Total _____/4

Shape Tank *(continued)*

Instruction sheet – Level 4

Game 3

Instructions

Score (✓ or ✗)

a   Select a hexagon, a circle, a square, a rectangle and a triangle.

b   Place the hexagon in the centre of the tank, and the square to the right of it.

c   Now place the triangle below the hexagon, and the circle above the hexagon.

d   Place the rectangle to the left of the hexagon, in the middle of the remaining space.

Total _____/4

Travel Game

You will need

Photocopies of the travel scene and score sheet pages

Scissors and a pen or pencil

How to play

Choose a scene, and present it to the child, talking him through the pictures to ensure that he is familiar with the vocabulary. Explain to the child that he will 'travel' through the scene, looking carefully at all the objects on the way. Help the child to link the objects together to create a story/visual picture in his mind. For younger children, cut out the mode of transport at the bottom of each scene: this can help the child to sequence their observations and recall.

After a few minutes, having created a story/visual picture, remove the scene from the child's sight and encourage him to recall the travel scene, naming aloud the specific objects from the scene, preferably in order. Record the child's pattern of recall on the score sheet.

Scene 1 – A Trip to the Zoo

Travel Game (continued)

Travel Game *(continued)*

Scene 2 – A Drive through Skarforth Town

welcome to
SKARFORTH TOWN

FRUIT & VEG

1
2
3
4
5
6

84

Scene 3 – Space Exploration

Travel Game *(continued)*

SPACE

1

2

3

4

5

6

Travel Game *(continued)*

Score sheet

Child's name _____ Date _____

Scene 1 – A Trip to the Zoo

Score (✓ or ✗)

1   Seal   ☐

2   Monkey   ☐

3   Giraffe   ☐

4   Banana tree   ☐

5   Bucket (of fish)   ☐

6   (Toilet) sign   ☐   Total _____/6

Scene 2 – A Drive Through Skarforth Town

Score (✓ or ✗)

1   Traffic lights   ☐

2   Mouse   ☐

3   Telephone (box)   ☐

4   People   ☐

5   (Fruit) shop   ☐

6   Streetlight/lamp post   ☐   Total _____/6

Travel Game *(continued)*

Score sheet

Child's name _____ Date _____

Scene 3 – Space Exploration   Score (✓ or ✗)

1 Moon ☐

2 Alien ☐

3 Planet ☐

4 Satellite (dish) ☐

5 (Floating) space helmet ☐

6 Meteorite and dust particles ☐   Total _____/6

Story Time

You will need

An age- or developmentally-appropriate story book
A photocopy of the recording chart

How to play

Select a story book that is unfamiliar to the child. Explain that you are
going to read the book (or part of it, depending on time available) and that
you would like him to try to visualise the important parts of the story in his
mind – using his internal camera. At the end of the story ask the child
some questions relating directly to the text. You can increase the difficulty
of questions to suit the child's ability. Record the number of correct
responses on the recording chart. Finally, ask the child to describe some
of his internal images – and then compare them to the actual pictures
in the book.

Story Time *(continued)*

Recording chart

Child's name _____ Date _____

Book title	Number of questions answered correctly
1	
2	
3	
4	
5	
6	
7	
8	
9	
10	
11	
12	

Drawing Game

You will need

Pencil, rubber and plenty of blank paper

Instruction sheet of an appropriate level

How to play

Read out each instruction, and encourage the child to listen carefully and then draw their response. The items must be drawn in the order that they are read out. There is no time restriction on this task, but encourage children to draw quickly, and to keep drawings basic – spending time adding detail can distract a child from repeating, which, in turn, leads to the instruction fading from memory.

Drawing Game *(continued)*

Instruction sheet

Child's name _____ Date _____

Level 1   Score (✓ or ✗)

Draw these things:

1	cat	mouse	fish	☐
2	pen	desk	book	☐
3	car	bike	boat	☐
4	tree	gate	flower	☐
5	moon	star	cloud	☐
6	watch	table	spoon	☐
7	window	stone	nail	☐
8	ladder	pen	leg	☐
9	key	ball	door	☐
10	spider	cup	egg	☐

Total _____/10

Drawing Game *(continued)*

Instruction sheet

Child's name _____ Date _____

Level 2   Score (✓ or ✗)

Draw these things:

1	bin	jug	flower	stick	☐
2	cat	pig	wall	leaf	☐
3	apple	sun	box	fork	☐
4	worm	bus	sock	hat	☐
5	pond	cup	bag	table	☐
6	snake	hill	house	grass	☐
7	finger	sun	pencil	brush	☐
8	spider	church	bike	boy	☐
9	rabbit	money	sand	box	☐
10	pen	chair	king	sock	☐

Total _____/10

Drawing Game *(continued)*

Instruction sheet

Child's name _____ Date _____

Level 3   Score (✓ or ✗)

Draw these things:

1	bridge	house	egg	clock	girl	☐
2	cloud	pen	square	hat	bell	☐
3	dog	grass	rain	car	phone	☐
4	ghost	pan	wheel	apple	grapes	☐
5	money	tree	window	ball	light	☐
6	jelly	door	path	boat	flag	☐
7	water	jumper	roof	stamp	nail	☐
8	umbrella	leg	arm	belt	fish	☐
9	nose	train	fire	bin	chair	☐
10	present	mirror	picture	candle	gate	☐

Total _____/10

Café Menu

You will need

Pen/pencil or counters

Photocopies of the menu pad pages

How to play

The adult acts as the customers, and the child as a waiter/waitress in a café. The customers give their orders, and the waiter/waitress must look, listen and then respond by marking the appropriate food on his menu pad. (Select the menu pad that is most familiar to the child.) Increase the length of the order as the child progresses, but be aware of how many foods you are expecting the child to remember. Younger children like different customers to have different voices!

Customers can only order food that is still available on the menu pad. Keep giving orders until all the food has been consumed!

Example

Waiter/Waitress:	'Can I take your order, please?'
Customer 1:	'Yes, I would like burger, fries and beans please.'
Customer 2:	'Em, I think I'll have pizza, … Er, no, burger with mushrooms and fries.'

REPEATING

WORKSHEET 12

Café Menu (continued)

Menu Pad One

Child's name _____   Date _____   Total correct _____

Mushrooms	Fish	Beans or Peas	Burger	Three sausages	Fried egg	Slice of bread
Three sausages	Burger	Fried egg	Two sausages	Mushrooms	Pizza	Fries
Kebab	Beans or Peas	Mushrooms	Fries	Burger	Beans or Peas	One sausage
Mushrooms	Fried egg	Fries	Kebabs	Beans or Peas	Fish	Slice of bread

Café Menu (continued)
Menu Pad Two

Child's name _____   Date _____   Total correct _____

White rice	Onion bhaji	Tandoori chicken	Samosa	White rice	Bombay potatoes	Lamb balti
Tandoori chicken	Onion bhaji	Samosa	Lamb balti	Naan	Vegetables	Tandoori chicken	Samosa
Popadom	Vegetables	Brown rice	Bombay potatoes	Chickpea dhal	Lamb balti	Naan	Curry
Balti	Vegetables	Popadom	Tandoori chicken	Naan	Chickpea dhal	Brown rice	Popadom

Picture Frames

You will need

A selection of coloured pens/pencils

Photocopies of the picture frame worksheet

Instruction sheets

How to play

Read out a set of drawing instructions from the appropriate level list. Once you have given the instruction, encourage the child (the artist) to draw his response within the picture frames. As with the drawing game (worksheet 11) there is no time restriction with this task. However, it is important to encourage the child to draw quickly and to keep drawings simple.

Time spent adding unnecessary detail can distract the child from repeating. The instructions vary in length, so select the length that the child needs most practice with – basic, medium or hard. Write the length type in the space provided at the top of each picture frame worksheet.

You may wish to enlarge the picture frames on the photocopier, before starting the game.

Picture Frames *(continued)*

Child's name _____ Date _____

Instruction type _____

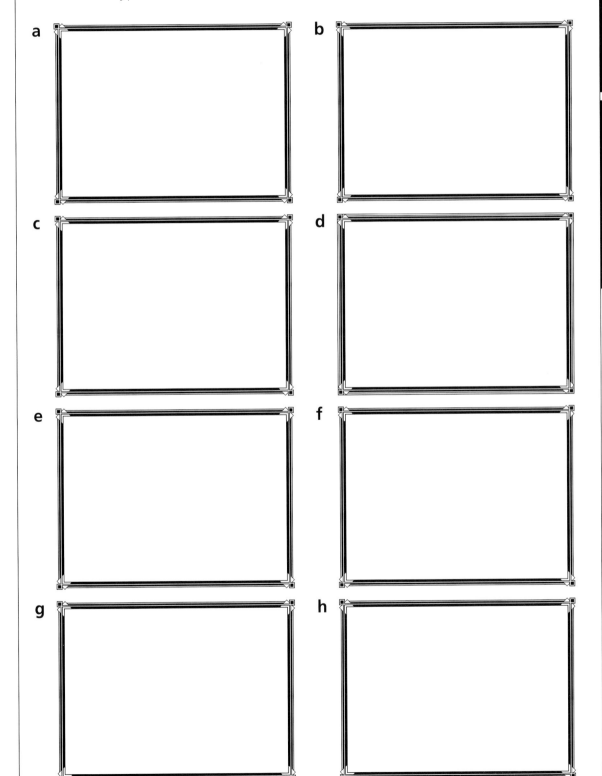

Picture Frames *(continued)*

Child's name _____ Date _____

Instruction type _____

i

j

k

l

m

n

Picture Frames *(continued)*

Drawing instructions

Basic

Draw: Score (✓ or ✗)

a   a boy, a girl and a cat.   ☐

b   a tree, a worm and rain.   ☐

c   some sand, the sea and a rock.   ☐

d   four red telephones.   ☐

e   a chair, a TV and a rug.   ☐

f   a table with a blue tablecloth.   ☐

g   a yellow car with a caravan.   ☐

h   a brown spider in its web.   ☐

i   a banana, an orange and an apple.   ☐

j   a book, a pen and a ruler.   ☐

k   some grass and a blue tent.   ☐

l   three flowers and a bumble bee.   ☐

m   a witch and two broomsticks.   ☐

n   a plate of egg and chips.   ☐

Total _____/14

Picture Frames *(continued)*

Drawing instructions

Medium

Draw: Score (✓ or ✗)

a   a red book with a hole in the corner.   ☐

b   a green bike with no handlebars.   ☐

c   a blue fish standing on its tail.   ☐

d   two sharks with blood on their teeth.   ☐

e   a boy running up a hill.   ☐

f   a farmer chasing a red duck.   ☐

g   a shop with a 'closed' sign in the window.   ☐

h   a set of traffic lights on green.   ☐

i   a blue car with a flat tyre.   ☐

j   three men in green stripy clothes.   ☐

k   a hand with a thumb and three fingers.   ☐

l   a man wearing sunglasses and a sunhat.   ☐

m   some smoke, a fire and a tree.   ☐

n   a blue radio on a blue table.   ☐

Total _____/14

Picture Frames *(continued)*

Drawing instructions

Hard (for the older child)

Draw: Score (✓ or ✗)

a   a hill with three people running down it. ☐

b   a night sky with an owl and some stars. ☐

c   a swimming pool with a red waterslide. ☐

d   a face with three eyes and one ear. ☐

e   four lines and a tiny circle. ☐

f   a cinema ticket with a hole in the top right-hand corner. ☐

g   a man holding a broken walking-stick. ☐

h   a grey CD, a blue and yellow battery and some coins. ☐

i   a straight line with a circle at either end. ☐

j   a bottle without a lid, containing blue liquid. ☐

k   two insects and two pieces of equipment used in sport. ☐

l   a yellow car with smoke coming out of the engine. ☐

m   something made of wood and something made of metal. ☐

n   a map – colour half of it red and half green. ☐

Total _____/14

REPEATING

WORKSHEET 14

Moving House

You will need

Photocopies of first- and ground-floor plans and furniture sheets

Boss's instruction sheet

A pen and a pair of scissors

How to play

Start by cutting out the furniture cards and sort by type of furniture. Place the floor plans and the groups of furniture cards in front of the child, making sure that the first-floor plan is directly above the ground-floor plan. Select the most appropriate level for the child, and read out the boss's instructions for that level. Encourage the child to respond by moving the furniture into the appropriate rooms. The child should be encouraged to wait until the instruction has been given in full, before responding. Record the child's responses on the boss's instruction sheet.

Gradually build up the level of difficulty as the child's memory strategies develop, clearing the furniture from each floor plan at the end of each level. Ensure that the vocabulary used in this game is familiar to the child – for example, establish whether the child uses the term 'living room', 'lounge', or 'sitting room', and adapt the boss's instructions accordingly.

Moving House (continued)

Ground-floor plan

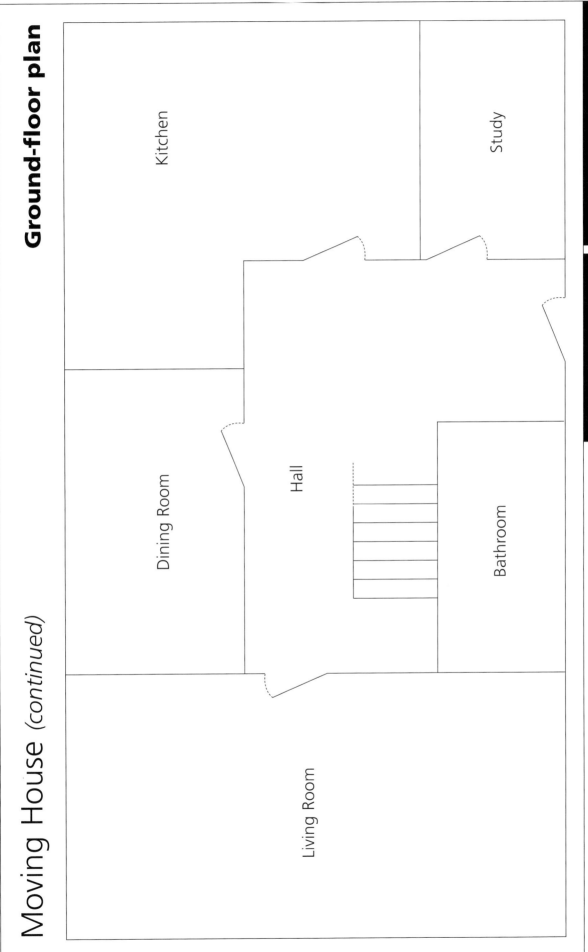

Kitchen

Study

Dining Room

Hall

Bathroom

Living Room

Moving House (continued)

First-floor plan

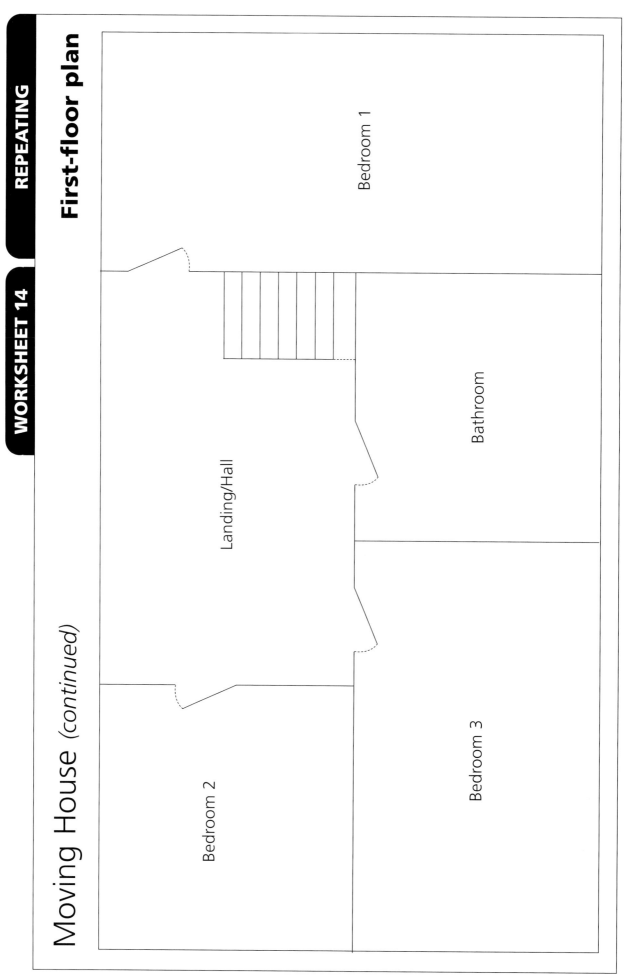

Bedroom 1

Bedroom 2

Bedroom 3

Landing/Hall

Bathroom

Furniture

Moving House *(continued)*

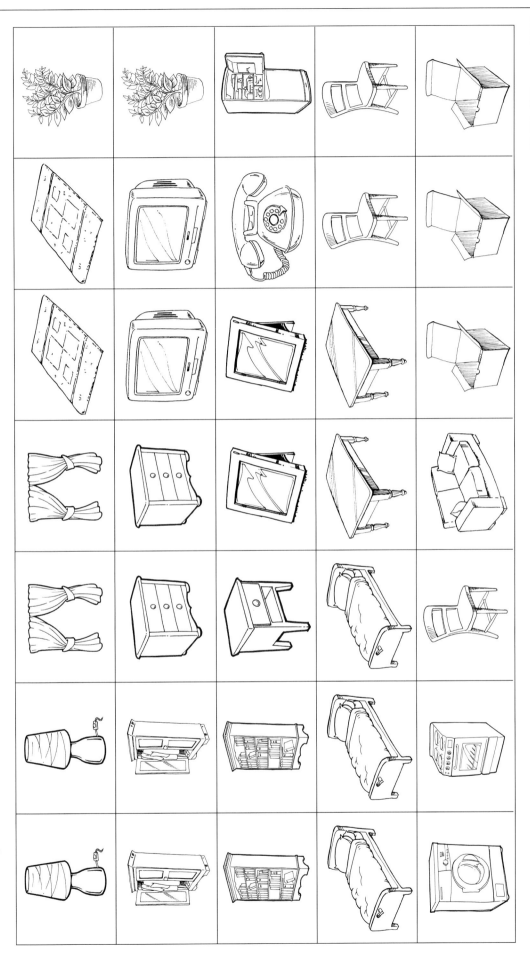

REPEATING

WORKSHEET 14

Moving House *(continued)*

Boss's instruction sheet

Child's name _____ Date _____

Level 1

Score (✓ or ✗)

1 Put a table and a sofa/settee in the living room. ☐

2 Put a mirror and a plant on the landing. ☐

3 Put a bed and a chest of drawers in a bedroom. ☐

4 Put a lamp and some curtains in a bedroom. ☐

5 Put a box and some curtains in a bathroom. ☐

6 Put a table and a bookcase in the dining room. ☐

7 Put a wardrobe and a chair in a bedroom. ☐

Total _____/7

Continue practice at this level by creating some additional instructions, or, if the child is able, progress to Level 2. Additional instructions should contain two objects and a room.

Moving House *(continued)*

Boss's instruction sheet

Child's name _____ Date _____

Level 2

Score (✓ or ✗)

1 Put a plant and a mirror in the downstairs bathroom. ☐

2 Put two chairs and a telephone in the study. ☐

3 Put two beds and a bookcase in bedroom 3. ☐

4 Put two boxes and a table in the hall. ☐

5 Put curtains and a plant in the upstairs bathroom. ☐

6 Put the washing machine, the fridge, and cooker in the kitchen. ☐

7 Put a chest of drawers and a wardrobe in bedroom 1. ☐

Total _____/7

REPEATING · WORKSHEET 14

Moving House *(continued)*

Boss's instruction sheet

Child's name _____ Date _____

Level 3

Score (✓ or ✗)

1 Put two rugs and a box in bedroom 1. ☐

2 Put a television, two mirrors and a sofa/settee in
the living room. ☐

3 Put curtains, a plant and a bed in bedroom 3. ☐

4 Put two beds and a chest of drawers in bedroom 1. ☐

5 Put a lamp, a chair, a bookcase and one box in
the study. ☐

6 Put a television, a table, the fridge and the cooker
in the kitchen. ☐

7 Put a table, two chairs and some curtains in the
dining room. ☐

Total _____/7

Watch Factory

You will need

A selection of coloured pens/crayons

Five photocopies of the 'factory stock' sheet and one of the boss's instruction sheets

How to play

You, as the adult, will be the boss at the watch factory, and the child is the skilled painter who paints the watches. The child has to listen carefully to their boss's instructions, then carry them out exactly on each watch themselves. You may wish to cut out the watches before you start the game. They can also be enlarged if required. Do not give the next design instructions until the child has completed the watch 'in hand'. Record the child's responses on the boss's instruction sheet.

Remember to select an appropriate level from the boss's instruction sheet. This game is only suitable for children who have an understanding of size, shape, colour, watch parts and plurals.

Watch Factory *(continued)*

Factory stock

Watch Factory *(continued)*
Boss's instruction sheet

Child's name _____ Date _____

Level 1 Score (✓ or ✗)

Watch 1
1 Colour the straps yellow. ☐

2 Colour the face blue. ☐

3 Colour the hands green. ☐

4 Colour the buckle red. ☐

Watch 2
1 Colour the face green. ☐

2 Draw ghosts on the straps. ☐

3 Colour the buckle green. ☐

4 Colour the ghosts yellow. ☐

Watch 3
1 Colour the winder red. ☐

2 Colour the hands blue. ☐

3 Cover the straps with dots. ☐

4 Colour over the numbers in green. ☐

Watch Factory *(continued)*

Boss's instruction sheet

Child's name _____ Date _____

Level 1   Score (✓ or ✗)

Watch 4

1   Put a football net on the face.   ☐

2   Colour the buckle black.   ☐

3   Put footballs on the straps.   ☐

4   Colour the hands black.   ☐

Watch 5

1   Colour the winder yellow.   ☐

2   Colour the hands red.   ☐

3   Put spiders on the straps.   ☐

4   Colour the buckle yellow.   ☐

Total _____/20

Watch Factory *(continued)*

Boss's instruction sheet

Child's name _____ Date _____

Level 2 Score (✓ or ✗)

Watch 1

1 Colour the big hand blue. ☐

2 Colour over two numbers in green. ☐

3 Colour over one number in red. ☐

4 Write your name on a strap. ☐

Watch 2

1 Draw stripes across the face. ☐

2 Put small stars on the straps. ☐

3 Colour one hand in red. ☐

4 Colour over three numbers in yellow. ☐

Watch 3

1 Draw three cobwebs on the face. ☐

2 Draw a fat spider on a strap. ☐

3 Colour both hands in black. ☐

4 Cover the other strap with ants. ☐

REPEATING

WORKSHEET 15

Watch Factory *(continued)*

Boss's instruction sheet

Child's name _____ Date _____

Level 2   Score (✓ or ✗)

Watch 4

1   Draw a happy clown on one strap.   ☐

2   Draw a circus tent on the face.   ☐

3   Draw balls on the other strap.   ☐

4   Colour over eleven numbers in yellow.   ☐

Watch 5

1   Draw stripes across the straps.   ☐

2   Draw dots between your stripes.   ☐

3   Colour the big hand red.   ☐

4   Colour the little hand blue.   ☐

Total _____/20

Watch Factory *(continued)*

Boss's instruction sheet

Child's name _____ Date _____

Level 3   Score (✓ or ✗)

Watch 1

1   Cover the face with little green squiggles.   ☐

2   Colour over the numbers nine and three in yellow.   ☐

3   Colour the buckle in green or yellow.   ☐

4   Colour the straps in big yellow squiggles.   ☐

Watch 2

1   Put thick blue stripes on the straps.   ☐

2   Put thin yellow stripes on the face.   ☐

3   Colour over the numbers six and twelve in red.   ☐

4   Colour over the numbers nine and three in blue.   ☐

Watch 3

1   Cover the face in lots of little raindrops.   ☐

2   Draw two colourful rainbows on a strap.   ☐

3   Colour over the numbers one and eight in red.   ☐

4   Colour the winder in red or blue.   ☐

REPEATING

WORKSHEET 15

Watch Factory *(continued)*

Boss's instruction sheet

Child's name _____ Date _____

Level 3   Score (✓ or ✗)

Watch 4

1 Cover the straps in little black squares. ☐

2 Cover the face in little green triangles. ☐

3 Colour the hands in green or black. ☐

4 Colour the winder in black and red. ☐

Watch 5

1 Colour the winder and hands in yellow. ☐

2 Colour over the numbers in yellow or blue. ☐

3 Draw three yellow mice on one strap. ☐

4 Draw two pieces of brown cheese on the face. ☐

Total _____/20

Watch Factory *(continued)*

Boss's instruction sheet

Child's name _____ Date _____

Level 4   Score (✓ or ✗)

Watch 1

1   Draw bumble bees flying in a row on the straps.   ☐

2   Colour the little hand in red or yellow.   ☐

3   Draw a big blue pot of honey on the face.   ☐

4   Colour the big hand in red or black.   ☐

Watch 2

1   Draw happy and sad faces on the straps.   ☐

2   Draw pink and brown feet over the face.   ☐

3   Colour over the numbers in any colour except green.   ☐

4   Colour half the winder in pink or brown.   ☐

Watch 3

1   Draw a thin yellow guitar on each strap.   ☐

2   Put little green music notes over the face.   ☐

3   Colour over the numbers in any colour except black.   ☐

4   Colour half the winder in yellow or green.   ☐

REPEATING

WORKSHEET 15

REPEATING

WORKSHEET 15

Watch Factory *(continued)*

Boss's instruction sheet

Child's name _____ Date _____

Level 4 Score (✓ or ✗)

Watch 4

1 Put three different colour flags on one strap. ☐

2 Draw the front half of a blue aeroplane on the face. ☐

3 Colour over the numbers with a colour used on one
of the flags. ☐

4 Colour the hands in any colour except red. ☐

Watch 5

1 Draw two long, grey broomsticks on a strap. ☐

2 Draw an old grey bubbling cauldron on the face. ☐

3 Draw green and yellow steam coming out of
the cauldron. ☐

4 Draw different coloured eyeballs over the second
strap. ☐

Total _____/20

Watch Factory *(continued)*

Boss's instruction sheet

Child's name _____ Date _____

Level 5   Score (✓ or ✗)

Watch 1

1 Draw a tall green christmas tree on one strap. ☐

2 Draw five presents on the face, of different sizes. ☐

3 Colour over the numbers three, six, nine and twelve in green. ☐

4 Colour over the other numbers in green, red, or blue. ☐

Watch 2

1 Draw a flower with pink petals and a yellow centre on the face of the watch. ☐

2 Draw lots of pink and red petals on one strap. ☐

3 Colour over the numbers five and three in orange. ☐

4 Colour over the numbers one, nine and eleven in yellow. ☐

REPEATING

WORKSHEET 15

Watch Factory *(continued)*

Boss's instruction sheet

Child's name _____ Date _____

Level 5   Score (✓ or ✗)

Watch 3

1 Colour the winder in any colour except red or green. ☐

2 Draw hamburgers of different sizes on one strap. ☐

3 Colour over the numbers in any colour except yellow
or red. ☐

4 Cover the face in thin, yellow fries. ☐

Watch 4

1 Draw a blue and grey spaceship landing on the face. ☐

2 Draw green and blue jumping aliens on the straps. ☐

3 Colour half the winder in grey and half in blue. ☐

4 Draw spacedust around the aliens and under the
spaceship. ☐

Watch Factory *(continued)*

Boss's instruction sheet

Child's name _____ Date _____

Level 5   Score (✓ or ✗)

Watch 5

1 Draw a yellow shark's fin on the face, with a tear
    in the fin.

☐

2 Draw different size bones over one strap, in grey.

☐

3 Put one dot of blood in the centre of each bone.

☐

4 Colour the winder in any colour except yellow
    or orange.

☐

Total _____/20

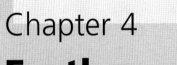

Chapter 4
Further resources

Short-Term Memory Difficulties
Advice Sheet for Teachers

The following guidelines may help a child with short-term memory difficulties, within the classroom setting.

1 Sit the child at the front of the class to aid concentration.

2 Ensure that the child is looking and listening before he/she is given an instruction.

3 Support verbal instructions/information with visual prompts – for example, write on the board, or at the top of the relevant page in the child's exercise book.

4 Keep verbal instructions/information concise – break instructions down into manageable stages, and repeat where necessary.

5 Continue to check the child throughout the lesson to ensure that he/she remembers the given task.

6 Self-esteem and confidence can often be low, so praise the child's successes frequently, however small.

7 When homework tasks are given verbally, provide a written account as well – this information needs to be remembered by the child at home several hours later!

8 Reassure the child that he/she is welcome to seek help, reassurance, or repetition of instructions during the lesson.

Short-Term Memory Difficulties
Advice Sheet for Parents/Carers

The following guidelines may help a child with short-term memory difficulties, within the home.

1 Ensure that your child is looking at and listening to you, before you give instructions/information.

2 Keep verbal instructions and important pieces of information concise – break instructions down into manageable chunks.

3 Support verbal instructions/information with natural hand gestures and facial expressions, wherever possible.

4 Be as patient as possible, and be prepared to repeat instructions/ information as and when your child requires.

5 Self-esteem and confidence can often be very low, so praise your child's successes frequently, however small.

6 Encourage your child to use a diary, chalk board, pin board, or an old notebook on a regular basis, to help them record and remember future events – for example, a friend's birthday party, sports' day, or bonfire night.

7 Reassure your child that it is acceptable to forget things from time to time – as we all do!

Memory Chart

MEMORY CHART

Child's name _____

Tick or colour the appropriate memory aid and strategy boxes used in each activity.

Activity	MEMORY AID AND STRATEGIES USED IN SPECIFIC ACTIVITIES							
	1 Repeating	2 Picturing	3 Writing or Drawing	4 Good Observation	5 Good Listening	6 Good Concentration	7 Asking For Help	8 Other
Picturing game								
Storytelling								
Telephone numbers								
Colouring game								
Action game								
Chinese whispers								
Bingo								
Shape tank								
Travel game								
Story time								
Drawing game								
Café menu								
Picture frames								
Moving house								
Watch factory								

Memory Strength Recording Chart

Child's name _____ Date started _____

Date and colour in the relevant box as the child achieves consistent recall.

MEMORY AND RECALL OF UP TO SIX DIGITS/PIECES OF INFORMATION

1 digit/piece of information	2 digits/pieces of information	3 digits/pieces of information	4 digits/pieces of information	5 digits/pieces of information	6 digits/pieces of information

Date _____ Date _____ Date _____ Date _____ Date _____ Date _____

Discussion and Drawing

You will need

Photocopy of the Matt Memory chart

Pen or pencils

How to play

Encourage the child to think of as many things as he can that may be used to help his memory. These may be things that he has seen other people use. Let the child draw his responses on the spaces of Matt Memory. Possible responses might include a diary, a calendar, a wall board, pen and paper, a notebook, observation/listening/concentration strategies, an adult's/friend's help, or a computer diary. Enlarge the chart on the photocopier to allow the child room to work.

The Following Things Can Help My Memory

Child's name _____ Date _____

'Hello, I'm Matt Memory.'

1	2	
3	4	5
6	7	8
		9

The Following Things Can Help My Memory

Child's name _____ Date _____ **digits/pieces of information now!**

I can remember _____

'Hello, I'm
Matt Memory,
and I'm getting
stronger and
stronger!'

6

5

4

3

2

1

Colour in the number of
pieces of information or digits
that you can now remember.

Memory Worksheet 1

Strategies

Encourage the child to answer the questions below.

1 Think of some strategies/aids that can help your memory.

1 _____

2 _____

3 _____

4 _____

5 _____

6 _____

2 Which one do you find works best?

_____

_____

3 Which one do you find least helpful?

_____

_____

Memory Worksheet 2

Scenarios

Encourage the child to think of ways to help his/her memory in the following situations.

1 Somebody rings to leave a message for your older sister. Your sister is out.

Method _____

_____

_____

2 You receive a birthday party invitation for next month.

Method _____

_____

_____

3 You have been asked to go to the shop to buy five items, but you do not have a shopping list.

Method _____

_____

_____

Memory Worksheet 2 *(continued)*

4 Your are queueing for a burger. Two of your friends have given you their orders and are waiting for you outside.

Method _____

_____

_____

5 You and a friend are meeting up in two weeks' time. You are to meet outside school at 7.45 pm.

Method _____

_____

_____

6 Your school library books need to be returned next Tuesday.

Method _____

_____

_____

7 A friend wants to borrow four of your favourite CDs. You rush home to get the CDs.

Method _____

_____

_____

Chapter 5

Assessments, resources, references and bibliography

Assessments

Bullock W & Meister Vitale B, 1987, *Ann Arbor Learning Inventory*, Ann Arbor Publishers, Belford.

Carrow-Woolfolk E, 1981, *Carrow Auditory–Visual Abilities Test (CAVAT)*, Teaching Resources Corporation, Hingham, MA.

Gathercole S & Baddeley A, 1996, *Children's Test of Non-Word Repetition*, The Psychological Corporation, London.

Newton M & Thomson M, 1976, *Aston Index*, LDA Park Works, Wisbech.

Pickering S & Gathercole S, 2001, *Working Memory Test Battery*, The Psychological Corporation, London.

Singleton CH, Thomas KV & Leedale R, 1996, *CoPS Cognitive Profiling System*, Lucid Research Ltd, Beverley.

Wilson BA, Cockburn J & Baddeley A, 1991, *The Rivermead Behavioural Memory Test*, Thames Valley Test Company, Bury St Edmunds.

Resources

Auditory Memory: Words in Pictures (WIP) 4, 1997, Black Sheep Press, Keighley.

Buzan T, 2001, *Use Your Memory*, Millennium edition, BBC Worldwide, London.

Kelly DA, 1995, *Central Auditory Processing Disorder: Strategies for Use with Children and Adolescents*, The Psychological Corporation, London.

Mitchell J, 1984, *Student Organiser Pack*, Communication and Learning Skills Centre, Sutton.

Mitchell J, 1994, *Enhancing the Teaching of Memory Using Memory Bricks*, Communication and Learning Skills Centre, Sutton.

Mitchell J, 1996a, *C Cards Manual*, Communication and Learning Skills Centre, Sutton.

Mitchell J, 1996b, *Mastering Memory*, Communication and Learning Skills Centre, Sutton.

Mitchell J, 2000a, *Time to Revise*, Communication and Learning Skills Centre, Sutton.

Mitchell J, 2000b, *Timely Reminders*, Communication and Learning Skills Centre, Sutton.

References and bibliography

Atkinson RC & Shiffrin RM, 1968, 'Human memory', Spence KW & Spence JT (eds), *The Psychology of Learning and Motivation*, Academic Press, New York.

Baddeley A, 2001, *Human Memory: Theory and Practice*, Psychology Press, Taylor & Francis Group, United Kingdom.

Baddeley A & Hitch JG, 1974, 'Working Memory', Bower GH (ed), *Recent Advances in Learning and Motivation*, Academic Press, New York.

Bartlett, FC, 1932/1995, *Remembering: A Study in Experimental and Social Psychology*, Cambridge University Press.

Bourtchouladze R, 2002, *Memories Are Made Of This*, Weidenfeld & Nicolson, London.

Craik IFM & Lockhart RS, 1972, 'Levels of Processing: a framework for memory research', *Journal of Verbal Learning and Verbal Behaviour* 11, pp671–84.

Cohen G, Kiss G & Le Voi M, 1999, *Memory: Current Issues*, Open University Press, Buckingham, Philadelphia.

Ebbinghaus H, 1885/1964, *Memory: A Contribution to Experimental Psychology*, Dover, New York.

Gathercole S, 1996, *Models Of Short Term Memory*, Psychology Press, London.

Gross RD, 1989, *Psychology: The Science Of Mind And Behaviour*, Hodder & Stoughton, London.

Hayes N, 2000, *Foundations Of Psychology*, Thomson Learning, London.

Squire LR, 1992, 'Declarative and nondeclarative memory: multiple brain systems supporting learning and memory', *Journal of Cognitive Neuroscience* 4, pp232–43.

Tortora G & Grabowski S, 1993, *Principles Of Anatomy And Physiology*, Harper Collins, London.

Wade C & Travis C, 1990, *Psychology*, Harper & Row, New York.